BEYOND

BEYOND ENGLISH

The missing pieces of your bi-lingual identity you won't learn at school

Anthony Fitzgerald
& Beata Holeckova

YOUCAXTON
PUBLICATIONS

ISBN 978-1-915972-39-2
Published by YouCaxton Publications 2024

YouCaxton Publications
www.youcaxton.co.uk

Dedicated to the memory of Alex Cameron KC, a quintessential Englishman who embodied the finest English values. This book is a tribute to him and the profound impact he had on Beata's journey.

'I'm Franciszek from Poland. Occasionally I have a problem with learning English. I can understand how to speak and read the language but sometimes I'm really confused about what the English really mean'.

Mirela: 'I'm from Romania; Sometimes the English seem to say one thing and it means something completely different. Who is able to understand this?'

Istvan: 'as a Hungarian I have problems with their humour. I sometimes just don't get those funny little remarks. They say the English have a dry humour but there's something else to it too.'

Sofia: 'in Spain we don't see the need to be as polite as the English are. They seem to say please, sorry, excuse me etc at every opportunity! Why do they feel the need to do it that often?

Jana: 'I'm Czech and I've really enjoyed learning English, but it's so difficult to understand the hidden meanings behind the language. You don't learn this at school, and people can't explain it to you. ***I wish there was a book that would help!'***

Contents

INTRODUCTION.

Why did we decide to write this little book?

Beata is an educational entrepreneur, a highly experienced and very successful teacher of English as a second language, and a neuro-encoding specialist. Originally from former Czechoslovakia, Beata started out as an average student, taking language classes in English with dreams of becoming fluent. After an eye-opening year in the UK in 1995 she emerged with a life-changing experience: near fluency in the language and it was clear to her that English was her passion. She began her English-teaching career in 2000 and has since worked with groups of multinational students of all abilities, ages and levels of skill. Her mission is to empower non-native English learners, enabling them to master the language, unlock their greatness, and forge a new, formidable, bilingual identity.

Anthony has been involved with language for a lifetime. He started as an advertising copywriter and then continued with his own advertising agency. He worked for Time Magazine with postings all over the world for nearly twenty years and has now become an Executive Coach to help people with their careers and their lives.

Beata's students, from many different countries, complained that although they were making great progress with learning the English language, they still did not understand the English completely. The hidden meanings, nuances and humour really confused them. It was almost as though there was a language within a language. Anthony has spoken that language and written about it for a lifetime and has lived in seven different countries, has sold in over forty countries and visited at least eighty countries. He's had to adapt his speaking and writing to suit audiences all over the world. This book was a natural partnership of needs and talents.

HOW TO BE AT HOME IN ENGLAND.

We'd like to be clear; this is NOT a book of instructions.

It's a brief outline of the ways that make the British, and perhaps more accurately the English, a little different in the way that they get on with each other, and the way that they communicate. It's also about strange English customs. It's about ways of thinking that may be quite different from the ways of thinking in your own country. It's about what the English like and what they don't like.

If you're reading this, you are probably someone who is studying, or have studied, English as their second language. You are making great progress with the English language, but you are still puzzled by daily verbal interactions that you don't begin to understand, that you don't find funny or don't even see the point of. Many of you come from societies who speak much more directly to each other, whose opinions are made abundantly clear and who use humour sparingly in general day-to-day conversation.

The United Kingdom (England, Northern Ireland, Wales, Scotland) is a country of over 67 million people with about 56 million of them living in England.

Although we can't generalise about them all, we want this book to be read by people who suspect that there is a standard of English behaviour and style that is recognisable around the world. It is much more evident in the older generations and amongst the better educated, and it certainly doesn't mean that everybody you meet in England is going to be like this, far from it – but there are a few things that almost everybody in the country abides by. One might characterise these aspects of English culture and language as being the best side of the English – and one that we think a lot of foreigners will want to find out.

To repeat, this book is not full of sweeping generalisations about all of the 67 million people in the United Kingdom of Great Britain and Northern Ireland; it is a book that is as close as possible to a description of middle-class England. And it is more than that: it describes in very broad terms what the English aspire to be and how they like to behave with each other, even if they don't always succeed.

This book will make it much easier for you to really understand what the English are saying to each other and to you. It will enrich your understanding and make life in general much easier as well.

All nationalities have their idiosyncrasies, their little expressions of character, and many of them are shared with other nationalities. We are not saying that the English are better or that their style of socialising or communication is better or worse than the style of any other nation. We are just pointing out some of the differences.

Most people learning English as a second language do so because they want to get to understand the country and be really understood and liked by its people. Let's face it, if you want to get on socially or in business, or if you want to find customers for your product or service, or learn to manage people, you should be able to understand more than just the words and grammar of a new language. You have to be able to recognise the emotions, beliefs, prejudices and feelings that make up the people you are trying to influence.

It's altogether possible that even people who already speak English as their home language or have English as the official second language in their country might learn something new. The list is long: Americans, Canadians, Pakistanis, Indians, Sri Lankans, Bangladeshis, South Africans, Australians, New Zealanders, West Indians, Hong Kong Chinese etc. A lot of them don't always find it easy to understand what the British are saying to them either, or indeed what the British are saying to each other.

It can take years to fully understand the English, but it needn't take so long if you keep an open mind and take into account the tips and ideas in these pages.

GEOGRAPHY AND HISTORY.

The first thing to remember is that the British are situated on a couple of islands separated from the Eurasian landmass by the sea. That creates a feeling of difference right away! It contributes in no small way to a different attitude.

The next thing is the fact that the origins of the English language are very confused. Originally the languages spoken on their island were of Celtic origin and then the Romans came between the 1st and 4th centuries and added Latin to the mix. After that, in the 5th and 6th centuries, the language became predominantly Germanic through Anglo-Saxon invaders from Germany, Denmark and the Netherlands. Then, in the 7th to 9th centuries, you add the languages of the Viking invaders from Norway, Sweden and Denmark. The big one was of course in 1066 when the Normans brought French into the language and French became the language of the ruling classes for nearly three centuries. It was all quite a mixture. Now add to this the influence of what was the British Empire. There is a significant influx of words from other cultures such as Hindi, Gujarat, Bengali, Sanskrit, Malay and Arabic.

The good side of it is that English has a huge vocabulary, arguably bigger than any other world language except possibly Mandarin Chinese; the bad side is that, because of its multifarious origins, it can be awfully difficult to learn the rules of English which can be downright confusing and illogical!

However we're assuming that you understand the difficulty and are persevering with your learning of this wonderfully expressive world language.

It's really worth appreciating that Britain has been welcoming immigrants for nearly a thousand years. Jewish refugees from the European continent in the 12th and 13th centuries and again from Russia in the 19th century and Germany in the 20th century. French Protestants, the Huguenots, in the 18th century and a considerable influx of German and Russian immigrants in the 19th century. Latterly, from the 19th century onwards, the Irish have been absorbed in huge numbers and West Indians and South-Asians in the second half of the 20th century. Now we are home to one in ten people born outside these islands and most are made to feel welcome by the vast majority of the indigenous population. Of course there are exceptions and there's no accounting for the small minority of any nationality who express unfriendly reactions, but, by and large, the British could be described as one of the most welcoming and tolerant people of any country in Europe.

It is also worth remembering that the British are, in part, descended from the warlike Vikings and, although most of them are welcoming, they are not always the most peaceable of people. They also spent a lot of the late Middle Ages raiding France, not to mention the piratical attacks on Spain and Portugal. As quite a warlike people, living as they do on a crowded island and all too easily roused to conflict, they have devised ways of diffusing and avoiding aggression and conflict amongst themselves.

This may well be the biggest reason for the way they use humour, understatement, fairness and why they avoid boasting, exaggeration and overclaiming.

Now let's try and understand together what the British are really saying to each other.

WHAT'S THE BETTER CLASS WAY OF COMMUNICATING IN ENGLAND?

A: Would you mind if I borrowed your pen for a moment?

B: Not at all, here you are. Anything else I can help you with?

A: No. Thank you so much. That's very kind of you to ask.

THE HIDDEN MEANINGS.

Avoiding confrontation.

Almost without exception all languages use and respect politeness as a way to initiate conversations, or as a way to go about life on a daily basis. The English tend to carry it to extremes. Almost all interactions seem to require the use of ‘Excuse me’, ‘Please’, ‘Yes please’, ‘Sorry’, ‘Thanks’, ‘No thanks’ or ‘Thank you’.

We do it automatically the whole time. We don’t even think about it but if the other person doesn’t follow the same ‘rules’ then a silent judgement is made! It’s important to say that none of these little verbal gestures of politeness should be over emphasised. They just slip out. They are used unselfconsciously. If you start exaggerating or over-emphasising them, there may be a suspicion that you are being sarcastic or mocking.

Here’s an example that most foreigners find absolutely bewildering! Imagine you are pushing your shopping trolley in the supermarket, and someone comes up behind you, absent-mindedly pushing into you. You respond instantly by saying ‘Sorry’ at the same time as the other person, the ‘guilty’ party says ‘Sorry’.

What is that all about! Well it’s basically the ‘injured’ party absolving the other person of blame reflexively so as to avoid any sort of conflict. It’s acknowledging instantly that the offending action was accidental.

A: Oh, do please excuse me! I’m so sorry for bumping into you.

B: No. No problem. I should have watched where I was going! So sorry.

Politeness.

Here's another example. You're talking to somebody in the street and a friend comes up. They are in a hurry and need to interrupt very briefly. They'll start with the word 'sorry' and then enter the conversation. This is usually accompanied by an apologetic facial expression. It's not really an apology but it is a way of saying 'I don't want to inconvenience you for a moment longer than necessary'. Without the 'sorry' it could be understood to be rather unfriendly.

Then there are over-elaborate phrases such as:

'I wonder would it be at all possible to...?'

'Might I trouble you to pass the salt?'

'I hope you'll forgive me, but I couldn't help but overhear...'

'I wonder, might I get past?'

These sort of phrases, and there are lots of them, may be used in situations where you don't know the other person very well and you want to signal good manners. You won't come across them too often in younger generations and they do sound a bit dated but when you do hear them accept them as extreme indications of politeness. You don't necessarily have to respond so elaborately!

That's what the use of polite words is generally about: the avoidance of conflict, the recognition of other people. These important little words make life smoother and easier. You will find that conversational exchanges with the English will get a bit easier if you use them and you will gradually be accepted as 'one of us'.

Just as in your own country it certainly doesn't hurt to use simple acts of politeness as well: holding a door for someone; making way for an older person; offering an older person a seat, etc.

Avoiding extremes.

After these basic building blocks, the better side of communicating with, and understanding, the English starts to become a bit more nuanced.

A: I was so sorry to hear the news about your husband.

B: Yes, but life must go on. The old boy will be missed.

The English shy away from extremes in language and that, in a way, covers the whole style of communication. A well-brought-up English person will rarely, if ever, show much emotion in public. When faced with appalling information, they are expected to show mild concern. A lot of people refer to that as 'stiff upper lip' which probably has its origins in the military, when soldiers were required to be unflinching under fire. Their long history of wars around the world probably accounts for this. To flinch under fire might be considered cowardly and weaken the confidence of those around you.

The same rule applies equally to receiving good news. A small smile of recognition on hearing that your son has won first prize at something and maybe a muttered 'well done, old boy' will usually be enough, in public. The celebrations may well go further at home. This rule is unlikely to apply to sporting events like football or rugby.

A: I've finished that project I've been working on. Here it is.

B: That's absolutely brilliant. You've done a really great job.

A: Oh, honestly, it's nothing really, I needed all the help I could get.

In general if one Englishman indicates any sort of praise to another it should be met with self-deprecating protestations. 'Really it was nothing', 'I can't take any credit', etc. Both parties are completely aware that honour has been satisfied. Recognition has been given and acknowledged without any boasting or undue emotion. And that brings us to humour.

Flattery and exaggeration.

The English are not good with flattery – they don't trust it – so if you want to indicate approval of an action or position taken then often a nod of approval is as far as you might go. In exceptional circumstances a short phrase such as 'that's rather a good result' or 'you must be pleased with the outcome' will usually be enough. There will be no need for embarrassed protestations of unworthiness, and you can both move on.

Exaggeration or over-claiming is to be avoided at all costs. The only exception is when exaggeration is used humorously. For instance, when referring to a long speech one might say: 'He went on for what seemed half a lifetime!' In general most English people can spot over-claiming and exaggeration a long way off. In general avoid words like, 'awesome', 'incredible' and 'fantastic'. It's always better to err on the side of under-statement, or at the very least, accuracy.

Not taking yourself too seriously.

A: I do believe that he is the most effective, charismatic and intelligent leader we could aspire to.

B: That's a bit over the top, isn't it?

There's nothing wrong with expressing sincere, firmly held views as long as they don't become loud or strident or, worse still, solemn. Over-sincerity can often sound solemn and most English people will think you are being pretentious and possible misleading. It is best not to praise too extravagantly or to agree, or disagree, too enthusiastically or loudly. Be serious and truthful to your views, but always leave a little room for the other person.

But worse still, solemnity can be very boring and being boring is a major crime to the better sort of Englishman.

Conversation at an intelligent level should always look to contain an element of entertainment. It's the best way to get listened to and the best way to get a point across without giving offence.

Humour.

Humour is, arguably the most important element in English communication. It is present in many, if not most, conversational exchanges even those involving serious subjects. It doesn't involve obviously funny jokes so much as little twists of humour involving an unexpected reaction or turn of events, or even a small play on words. Humour is used to make potentially bad or critical news palatable, to admit that there are always two sides to everyone's story, to take the steam out of a controversial view, to let the other person know that you are not taking yourself too seriously, and many more such scenarios. (The biggest turn-off is to be seen to take yourself too seriously!) The list is long.

Mostly the humour used in casual conversation is light and throw away and should not be taken personally. It is just another tool of conversation that makes communication easier and is almost always friendly in intent.

It will take a long time and a lot of listening before you may be able to use humour in English in the same way. Be patient and it will start to come naturally and bring you and your listener much more enjoyment in conversation and social interaction.

Irony and sarcasm.

One of the basic elements of humour is irony, and its slightly more aggressive cousin, sarcasm. It usually involves saying the opposite of what is intended and serves to emphasise disagreement or suggest that the conventional or expected view is ridiculous. You've got to be aware of the context and this requires careful listening and having a little understanding of both the subject and the expected views of the other person in the conversation. As a non-native speaker it can be difficult to spot. Context is everything. Nine times out of ten, irony and sarcasm are used to raise a smile and not to cause offence.

Word games.

Double meaning. Innuendo. Playing on words. Most languages will incorporate these as part of their normal, colloquial style. They are endless amongst the English. A lot of it is facetious i.e. attempting to be funny for the sake of it, which can be quite irritating. There's so much depth to the English vocabulary that there's always an opportunity for you to play on words and take advantage of double meanings. Also many English people can't resist the use of puns, and the worse the pun the funnier it is. All these devices are designed to bring entertainment into the conversation. They make conversation flow lightly.

A: Did you hear about Fiona's new job?

B: Oh yes, she's certainly climbing the ladder.

A: Well, she always had a knack for reaching new heights.

The indirect approach.

It can be confusing when you hear opinions and judgements expressed in a way that doesn't sound enthusiastic. As far as you can see, the other person has done something remarkable or at least worthy of praise, yet you'll hear it downplayed. 'Not bad' can mean very good, 'Nice' can be beautiful, 'Can't complain' might mean you really like it!

A: Not bad out today.

B: Yes, it's quite mild for this time of year. Pouring it down tomorrow I expect.

The British use the subject of weather as a way of opening conversation or of indicating that they recognise you as a fellow human being! It's the ultimate in the indirect approach. The weather as a subject is so safe because, being on an island on the edge of an ocean, it can change five or six times in a day. You can say absolutely anything about the weather and, if practised, can use it to pivot into other subjects. A muttered remark as you enter a pub or cafe such as 'it's raining cats and dogs out there' will just signal that you're part of the group in recognising a common acceptance.

Foreign accents.

We probably don't need to point out that not everybody in England tolerates foreign accents, foreign appearance and different ethnicity. We think you'd have to agree that there's an equally sizeable proportion of the population in your own country of origin that is equally intolerant. But remember that we are trying to illustrate how the best of the English behave, not the worst of them.

Without being guilty of over-claiming and allowing for everybody's personal experiences, it is probably fair to say the England is a country that accepts and tolerates more nationalities, accents, religious choices and ethnicities than most. The very fact that we are a small and crowded island means that we have to be tolerant; the alternative is chaos. The English are a pragmatic people. They act, like everybody else, in their own interest and it is quite clear to most people that we are all going to live easier and more fulfilling lives if we embrace differences.

British accents.

A: Oi, mate, 'd'yasee the footie last night?

B: Nah, missed it. Ow'd it go?

A: T'was a cracker, ended in a draw, mate!

Most of you will have problems understanding British accents unless you learn your English in one particular region with very distinctive accents (Manchester, Birmingham, Liverpool, Newcastle, Glasgow for example) and only hear that one accent.

We are sure that the country where you were brought up originally has the same situation, to a greater or lesser extent, so you should recognise the problem.

Not so many years ago you could say that there were literally hundreds of regional accents in the British Isles. A lot of the British could barely understand each other. Even today, a Londoner trying to understand somebody from Liverpool, Newcastle or Glasgow, and vice versa, can face real problems. The differences are still very marked – Scottish, Northern Irish, Welsh, the Midlands and the North of England in particular, proudly retain their unique differences – but there are nowhere near as many regional differences as before.

We are looking at finding the best side of the English, the side that the rest of the world finds acceptable and endearing. Generally, the best of the English language is conveyed by what is known as 'R.P.' or 'Received Pronunciation'. It is spoken by the privately educated and the children and the grandchildren of the privately educated. It is spoken generally by the land-owning class. It is also spoken by those who have come through the top universities and those who have risen to the top in the professions, the civil service and in the financial world, regardless of their earlier education. But be very aware that somebody with a regional accent can be just as well educated. They just choose not to betray their early roots out of pride and strength of character.

Received pronunciation is, without doubt the accent that offers the most clarity, the one that will get you through the most doors and will indicate that you are to be taken seriously in whatever profession or career path you choose.

Idiom, slang and jargon.

All languages, including English, have different layers of speech and understanding that goes way beyond what you might learn initially. Let's define them and remember that there are literally hundreds of examples in each category.

Idiom (really useful in context).

Idioms are phrases or expressions whose meanings cannot be understood from the literal meanings of their individual words. They often have cultural or contextual significance which may not be easily understood by those not familiar with the language or culture. A few examples of the literally hundreds of idiomatic expressions:

Bite the bullet: *To endure a painful or difficult situation.*

Break a leg: *Wishing someone good luck especially in a performance event.*

Break the ice: *To initiate a conversation.*

Burn the midnight oil: *To work late into the night.*

Cost an arm and a leg: *To be very costly.*

Cry over spilled milk: *To dwell on past mistakes that can't be undone.*

Hit the hay: *Going to bed or going to sleep.*

Jump on the bandwagon: *To adopt a popular activity or trend.*

Kick the bucket: *Someone dying.*

Piece of cake: *Something that's easy to do.*

Spill the beans: *To disclose a secret.*

The cat's out of the bag: *A secret has been revealed.*

Slang (often only used by the young but some expressions in general use).

Informal words, phrases and expressions used in casual conversation. Slang is informal, creative and evolves very quickly. Newly invented words, altered meanings of existing words, abbreviations and expressions not recognised in formal language. A few examples:

Chill: *Relax or take it easy.*

Dope: *Excellent or cool.*

FOMO: *Fear of missing out.*

Gonna: *Short for 'going to'.*

***Sick**: Awesome or impressive.*
***Ghosted**: Ignored or suddenly stopped communicating.*
***Scrummy**: Delicious.*
***Skive**: Avoiding work or responsibilities.*
***Sussed**: Figured out or understood.*
***Loo**: Toilet or bathroom.*
***Telly**: Television.*
***Quid**: Pound (currency).*
***Rizz:** Ability to charm or woo.*

Jargon.

Specialised language used within specific professions, industries or groups, often using technical terms and difficult to understand without specific background knowledge. There are medical, legal, IT, academic, financial, aviation, engineering, sports, marketing, scientific, military, environmental, telecommunications, fashion industry and human resources jargons.

A few examples:

***MRI (Magnetic Resonance Imaging):** A medical imaging technique.*
***Subpoena:** A legal document requesting appearance in court.*
***Firewall:** A security system between networks.*
***ROI (Return on Investment):** Measuring the profitability of an investment.*
***Pedagogy**: The method and practice of teaching.*
***Hedge Fund:** An investment fund that pools capital.*
***Hat Trick:** When a player scores three goals in a single game.*
***AOR:** Area of responsibility.*

Biodiversity: *The variety of plant and animal life.*
Bandwidth: *Maximum rate of data transfer across a network.*

What the British say and what they mean.

As an example of how confusion can arise when listening to what the English say take a look at this fairly light-hearted list of business language misunderstandings.

Not to be taken too literally or too seriously!

What the British say	What the British mean	What others understood
I hear what you say.	*I disagree and do not want to discuss it further.*	*He accepts my point of view.*
With the greatest respect.	*I think you are an idiot.*	*He is listening to me.*
That is a very brave proposal.	*You are insane.*	*He thinks I have courage.*
That's not bad.	*That's good.*	*That's poor.*
Quite good.	*A bit disappointing.*	*Quite good.*
I would suggest.	*Do it or be prepared to justify yourself.*	*Think about the idea but do what you like.*
Oh, incidentally/by the way.	*The primary* purpose of our *discussion is...*	*That is not very important.*
I was a bit disappointed that	*I am annoyed that...*	*It doesn't really matter.*
Very interesting.	*That is clearly nonsense.*	*They are impressed.*
I'll bear it in mind.	*I've forgotten it already.*	*They will probably do it.*

I'm sure it's my fault.	*It's your fault.*	*Why do they think it's their fault?*
You must come for dinner.	*It's not an invitation, I'm just being polite.*	*I'll get an invitation soon.*
I almost agree.	*I don't agree at all.*	*He's not far from agreement.*
I only have a few minor comments.	*Please re-write completely.*	*He has found a few typos.*
Could we consider some other options?	*I don't like your idea.*	*They have not yet decided.*

What the British talk very carefully about.

These three subjects of conversation can be tricky in England. Of course everybody has a view and an opinion, but all three topics are considered private. It doesn't mean that you can't bring them up but be careful about expressing your opinions too forcefully or asking too many direct, personal questions. You can still learn a lot by using an impersonal and indirect style.

Religion.

Religion is usually difficult because arguably the UK is living in an era of diminishing practising-Christianity despite professing to be a Christian country. The established religion is the Church of England (C of E), part of the overall European Reformation in the 16th century. It renounced papal authority under Henry VIII (1519 to 1547) and its doctrines stem from Martin Luther's '95 Edicts' in Germany. Most English will say that they are C of E, but a strikingly low proportion actually practise the religion by attending church. That in part accounts for the embarrassment in talking about it!

All religions are tolerated. National census figures from 2021 indicate 46.2 percent of the population in England and Wales are Christian. Of the remaining population, 6.5 percent identify as Muslim; 1.7 percent as Hindu; 0.9 percent as Sikh; 0.5 percent as Jewish; and 0.5 as Buddhist. The rest are likely to be largely agnostic or atheist. There are strict laws and penalties against discrimination on the grounds of religion, and Islamophobia and Anti-Semitism can be treated as hate crimes.

Politics.

Political views must be treated respectfully in the UK. The present House of Parliament (as at December 2023) has 357 Conservative MPs, 196 Labour MPs, 44 Scottish National Party MPs, 15 Liberal Democrat MPs with 24 MPs spread amongst 7 smaller parties.

A summary is that Labour voters tend to come from working class origins with many socialist ideas and the party stands for a greater distribution of wealth and power. It favours state protection of all citizens and a tax system that diminishes the gap between rich and poor. It has a strong following in the Midlands and the North of England. The Conservatives tend to favour less government with less taxation, a market-driven economy, private ownership and the holding of power by people selected on merit.

You should always be conscious of the fact that among both Labour and Conservative voters that there is a significant proportion who would never dream of changing parties. They are likely to follow the voting habits of their parents, their grandparents and even their great grandparents! Tread carefully and if you are new to this country only ask for information in a neutral and non-committal way.

Sex.

The British just don't talk about it much. The change in attitude in just a few decades is fairly remarkable with the now almost complete acceptance of equality of the sexes. However, it is still something that people don't talk about much and when they do it will be treated, like everything else, with humour. Enjoy it but don't chatter away about it!

WHAT'S THE BETTER CLASS WAY OF BEHAVING IN ENGLAND?

BEHAVIOUR AND VALUES.

To understand the British a little better you should be aware of some dos and don'ts that may not be evident in the country you come from. There will be many things that you might think are done better in your home country, but if you want to really understand life in Britain you should be aware of some differences.

Fairness.

Moving away from language but still essential, is to understand the way the English think and, crucial to this is the concept of *fairness*.

Fairness implies equal treatment in any situation. As an example look at most London traffic scenarios: in a traffic jam one car will nudge forward from the right. It will be followed by one car from the left. Followed in turn by a car from the right. No horn has been heard and only small signs, such as a nod or a finger raised in acknowledgement, will affect the process. It is understood by everybody in the traffic jam that the best and most efficient way to keep the traffic moving is to act fairly i.e. in turn. Now contrast that with traffic behaviour in most European countries where commonly every car is attempting to get into the same space at the same time. It is actually only reflecting what most of the English expect of life.

The other classic example of fairness is queuing. It's almost a joke but the English will make an orderly queue for everything, and you'd be well advised to wait your turn in the queue. It's all about fair behaviour or behaving with others as you'd like them to behave with you. Of course everybody is basically self-interested but in situations where the outcome will be improved by cooperation the English will go for fairness every time. This word also applies to the accepted norms of behaviour, i.e. if society has accepted that things are done in a certain way, by tradition or usage, most English will accept that.

Punctuality.

An important part of politeness is punctuality. The better sort of English person takes punctuality quite seriously. This applies to any situation, social or business. Of course unavoidable delays of five or ten minutes are always understood, but beyond that it would be considered rude not to let the other person know that you'll be delayed. The only exception is for an invitation to a dinner party at someone's home where you will be expected to be ten to fifteen minutes late. The idea being that you are giving your host a little more time in case things are going wrong.

One of the basic building blocks of higher quality English language interaction has to lie with the use of these simple words and acts of politeness and punctuality.

Class.

Let's talk about class. Quite honestly, we believe that the rest of the world takes the subject of the British class system more seriously than it does itself.

Class difference used to be a lot more important and lot more recognisable than it is today. Differences do still exist, and the most obvious outward difference is accent. However, a large section of the public will now boast openly of their working-class origins. It implies honesty, integrity, ambition and a hard-working attitude. Quite a lot of these people have in fact transitioned to a more comfortable existence and lifestyle and could be described now as middle-class. They still want to let you know that their values remain unchanged and that they are not 'traitors' to their original class (and parents). The actual working class still speak with metropolitan or rural accents and may be only educated to a limited level. They are in industrial, rural and manual jobs. The urban accents are usually spoken very quickly (as with most urban accents round the world). You can find it difficult to keep up with urban accents like Cockney (London), Scouse (Liverpool), or Geordie (Newcastle). The niceties of the English language style won't generally relate to them, but some very basic characteristics do, and they are important: humour, a sense of fairness, basic politeness, honesty in speech.

The middle class is so broad that it defies definition. At one end it comprises people who are reasonably comfortably off, educated to high-school graduate level and speak in muted regional accents and at the other end, people who are living very comfortably, are well-educated, and speak RP (Received Pronunciation) English.

Which leaves us with the upper class. How do you define an upper-class English person? The nearest certainty is that they will speak with an RP accent. Great attention is given to courtesy and good manners although they can be used to deceive. They will probably have inherited money and/ or property. They will NOT necessarily be educated to university level although in this day and age that is more likely. They will generally display a confidence and bearing that has been instilled into them by parents and schools.

If you feel you have to define a person by their class, the only safe way of judging class is by accent, and that means that an impoverished and unemployed young man living in a one-room flat who speaks with an RP accent is quite possibly an upper-class gentleman who has fallen on hard times; it also means that a big, good-looking, well-dressed fellow splashing cash around at a charity dinner and speaking with a mild 'Estuarine' accent is very far from being upper class. By the way, an 'Estuarine' accent is usually accepted as a universal southern accent covering all of the south-east of England with its roots in London Cockney and Essex cockney accents. It transcends its working- and middle-class origins, but it can be spoken quickly which can make it difficult for foreigners to understand.

Class consciousness is diminishing but it still exists. Judgements are still made about people's behaviour, how they dress, where they went to school and how they sound. However it is not as important as it used to be. As a foreigner the only sign of class that you can project is by thoughtful, polite and intelligent behaviour. That's what real class is about anyway!

Raising children.

This is a sensitive issue for every parent regardless of where they come from. First off, physical punishment of children, at home or at school, is prohibited by law in Britain. You may notice that there is a culture that encourages praise for children rather than criticism or punishment. In most of the state schools, competition in sports has nearly vanished, the theory being that competition prevents less physically able pupils from feeling unequal or makes them feel discriminated against. Competitive sport flourishes in private schools.

Most schools have compulsory school uniforms which promote discipline and are shown to lower noise levels and lead to significantly better listening from pupils. They also serve to hide any social differences between pupils.

In general schools are pretty tough on pupils wearing jewellery or having dyed hair.

Something that can amuse people from some countries is the emphasis placed on table manners. It has to be said that most countries will share these. You'll often hear mothers telling children to '*take their elbows off the table!*', '*don't talk with your mouth full*', '*ask permission to get down from the table*' etc. Some of the instructions seem a bit unnecessary but it's just one of the ways that parents try to raise their children to be more co-operative human beings.

Volunteering.

There is a very welcome culture of volunteering in Britain. There are examples of this everywhere: in the running of food banks, working at health centres, being teaching assistants, doing charity work and lately taking in refugees, particularly from Ukraine. We are not saying for a moment that people don't volunteer in other countries; of course they do but it is very much in evidence in Britain as part of the culture. If you are able to volunteer, even in a minor way, it could really accelerate your ability to fit into English society.

Bribery and corruption.

You are sure to welcome the knowledge that it is almost impossible to find anyone to bribe in this country! Be they police, civil servants, teachers, doctors etc as can happen in some countries. We wouldn't say that bribery and corruption doesn't take place in Britain. Of course there are occasionally examples of corruption within local government (particularly planning) but at a level that is very unlikely to affect your daily life. It also has to be said that when it is uncovered it has pretty unfortunate consequences for the people involved. It really is not part of British culture.

Policing.

There's been much criticism about the lack of physical presence of the police on the streets. It's partly due to the different nature of modern crime but the police still retain all the authority that is needed and without carrying arms. Gun-control laws are in force and are observed. The rule of law does generally prevail and most of us feel relatively safe in our beds!

WHAT THE BRITISH LIKE DOING.

Drinking tea.

Some people say that tea drinking won the last war! It punctuates life in Britain. It's taken as a reward for hard work; it's regarded as soothing and relaxing; it fills embarrassing moments; it's democratic. Everybody loves a 'cuppa' – that's shorthand for 'a cup of tea.' Of course coffee has made great inroads into the British way of life and coffee shops are everywhere, but it just isn't the same in the national psyche. You don't have to switch your beverage just to fit in, but it might be helpful to you to understand how important tea is. You could even get to like it yourself... with milk of course, not a slice of lemon!

Owning pet animals.

Be very aware that the English can sometimes attach more importance to the treatment of animals than to the treatment of their fellow humans. We know that sounds a little crazy, but the explanation lies again in their sense of fair play and justice. An animal, be it a horse, a dog or a cat, provides companionship . It needs to be fed, sheltered and exercised and beyond that it can't do much to help itself if injured or deserted. It's widely understood that human beings have a responsibility to an animal's well-being. People who mistreat animals in any way are regarded generally with contempt. If you show appreciation for someone's pet, you are showing appreciation for the owner and their values. It's a great conversation starter too!

Playing and following sport.

It's generally known that the English, for unaccountable reasons, appear to have invented most of the world's sports. Or if they haven't actually invented some of them, they created the rules for a large number of them. In the winter there is football (Soccer or Association Football as it's formally known) and rugby (Rugby Union Football using an oval ball) with football having many more participants and followers. There is also Rugby League football played mostly in the north of England which is slightly different to Rugby Union. Curiously the rough and very physical game of rugby is more often played by the privately educated and the middle class.

However, the most popular game here, as in most of the rest of the world, is the round-ball game of football. You'll find great loyalty to individual teams expressed by just about everybody even if they've never been to a match. It is a great conversation starter, and you could do worse than find a team to support and learn a little bit about them. Then in the summer it is cricket. We are not going to tell you how cricket is played in these pages, but you could do worse than get a friendly English friend to describe it to you. It's great conversation starter if you can even begin to understand the rules and the loyalties to different teams.

Drinking in pubs and cafes.

The British do like a drink or two. Some will say we drink too much, but actually we are about in the middle of the rankings in Europe as far as alcohol per capita is concerned.

The British pub is rightly famous as an institution where you meet people from all walks of life and put the world to rights. A pub is certainly a great place to meet the natives and improve your language.

If you too like a drink, then one or two visits a week should enable you to fit in beautifully. Wine bars and cafes with licences are also worth a try. It depends on your attitude to healthy drinking and one or two pints of bitter or glasses of wine should be enough for most people. Avoid the apparently growing tendency of the younger generations to binge drink – that way can lead to disaster and, as a foreigner, to arguments you are unlikely to win!

Loving the great outdoors.

If you manage to get out of the cities, you'll find that the English countryside is as beautiful as anywhere on earth. The trouble is that the weather is completely unpredictable. It doesn't stop the English though and it shouldn't stop you. Even in the city, as soon as the sun comes out, you'll find people laying out picnics in the park and rather amazingly actually baring themselves to the sun in the forlorn hope of getting a tan!

The right to roam is not as extreme as, say, in Sweden, but public footpaths are everywhere in Britain and the public's right to wander on them unobstructed creates the most wonderful opportunities to see and enjoy this often beautiful country.

There is a genuine love of the outdoors among the British, and it shows itself in the national obsession with gardening. Even with just a small patch of lawn you'll find many English almost obsessed with making their gardens look beautiful. That's why there are so many gardening programmes on television. If it's something you're drawn to, then start digging and you'll find kindred spirits.

Franciszek: 'Now I understand. I've had some really good conversations with some of my English colleagues by just thinking about some of these tips. It was interesting to hear what they thought about it.'

Jana: 'I found that if I stopped being too formal and serious and threw in some extra polite words, I started to get to know people much better. They started talking to me more openly and it gave me the confidence to do the same.'

Mirela: 'Yes, they seemed to trust you more and treat you as an equal if you keep it light, didn't get too emotional, talk about the weather, and looked for the humour in every situation.'

Istvan: 'I've got a lot more to learn, but now that I understand the reasons behind why the English talk to each other the way they do, I find my actual language, and even my accent, starts to improve.'

FINAL THOUGHTS.

So learn from the better side of the English by being polite and punctual, underplay your achievements, don't be too boastful, find humour whenever you can, make your conversation entertaining, acknowledge your mistakes, speak slowly and smile a bit and you will find that most British are tolerant, welcoming and forgiving. And remember that you can always fall back on the weather!

We must repeat, again and again, that this small book can never be completely accurate because our society is changing daily. The youth keep innovating language and habits; newcomers, maybe like yourselves, add elements of their own cultures. It can best be summed up by saying that it is how the 'middle-of-the-road' English understand each other and how they expect each other to behave, in very broad terms.

It is an attempt to help you understand the British, and particularly the English, a little better. It won't help you with all elements of our society, but it is a way of talking , a way of understanding and a way of behaving that will make your life a little easier and a little more enjoyable. It poses no threat to your national identity of which you must be rightly proud, but it does allow you to be able to switch from one identity to another without offending anyone.

It is our sincere wish that you will master the English language and speak it with confidence and ease, that one day you may choose to make England your adopted country and that you understand and even like the English people and be liked in return. We are both proud to call this country home.

If you are inspired to go further in mastering English, and forging a new bilingual identity, then consider joining Beata's Beyond English Academy. www.beataholeckova.com

Be part of a global community, and access weekly language and mindset coaching to take your English language and persona to the next level.

Additionally, if you are at a career crossroads and interested in executive and managerial development visit www.anthonyfitzgeraldcoaching.com

Anthony is happy to have a free conversation to discuss what you might need. A significant discount will be available on his fees for anyone signed up to Beata's Beyond English Academy.

9781915972392

BV - #0035 - 060125 - C0 - 203/133/3 - PB - 9781915972392 - Matt Lamination